Luna & Me

The True Story of a Girl
Who Lived in a Tree to Save a Forest

Jenny Sue Kostecki-Shaw

Christy Ottaviano Books
Henry Holt and Company
NEW YORK

Have you ever climbed a tree?
And stayed there **ALL** night?

Once there was a girl
who **LIVED** in a tree —
for over **TWO** years!

Nearly a thousand years ago, a redwood tree named Luna sprouted on a hillside. She grew up in a big family with strong roots.

Julia was born some thirteen thousand full moons later. Her family was always moving.

Upon arriving in each new town, she scurried off to explore the forests.

She whispered her secrets to the animals.
And soon the animals trusted Julia.

Once, a butterfly rested on her finger ALL day, which was how she got her nickname—Butterfly.

Luna, the redwood tree, held butterflies, too—and wise spotted owls, friendly banana slugs, gentle turkey vultures, daring flying squirrels, shy foxes, and a menagerie of forest friends.

Luna often reassured the animals:

If my arms seem full, it is not a chore.
I will gladly grow more!

And she always did.

One day, Butterfly wandered into an ancient cathedral of redwoods. Her heart beat wildly.

Thump . . .
a-thump . . .
a-thump . . .
a-thump!

"Hello?" a curious Butterfly called up into Luna. "Is anyone home?" Broken branches stuck out of Luna's trunk like porcupine quills, and her side was tagged with a blue **X**.

The redwood quivered with excitement,
the way she always did when
a new visitor arrived.

Luna thought,
Do you like to
climb trees?
Give me a try,
oh please!

All aflutter,
Butterfly called
out, "Here
I come!"

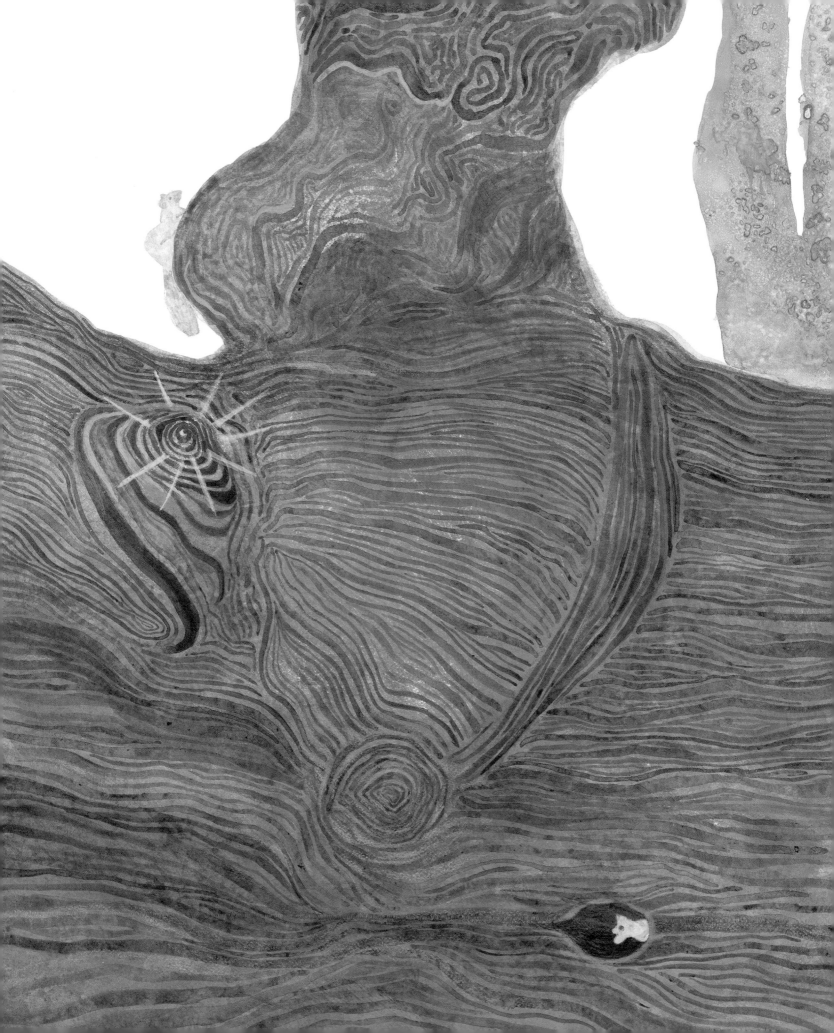

When she reached a comfortable perch, Butterfly introduced herself.

"I am Butterfly. And **YOU**, Luna, are a ladder to the MOON!"

Luna smiled inside.
Welcome, little Butterfly.
You are brave to have ventured up so high!

Butterfly marveled at Luna's view of the world.

She spied a river twisting this way and that past Luna's countless brothers and sisters and cousins.

But then she looked closer.

Butterfly's spirit wilted.
She knew that people needed
wood for building houses and
wood for building houses and
furniture—and for making
paper and books, too. But trees
make the oxygen we breathe,
she thought.

Animals need trees for
their homes. And without
tree roots, mountainsides can
wash away in heavy rains.
Don't trees have a right
to just be?

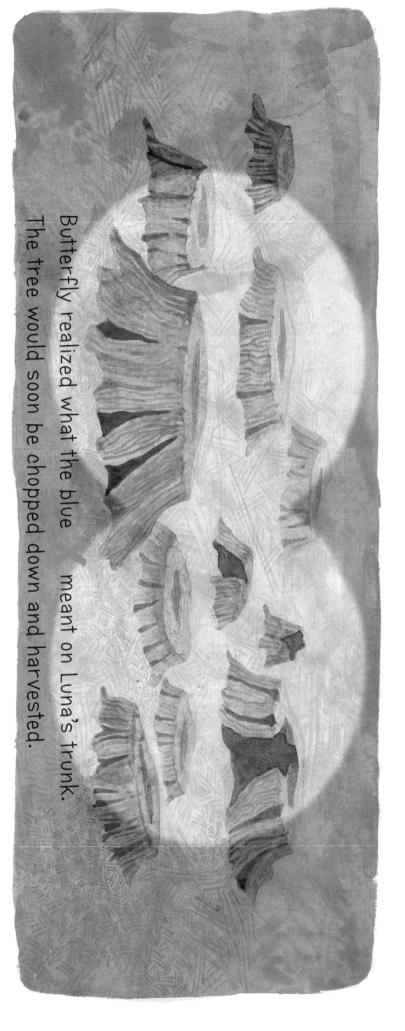

Butterfly realized what the blue   meant on Luna's trunk.
The tree would soon be chopped down and harvested.

Suddenly, an idea sprouted deep inside Butterfly. "If I stay with Luna, no one will cut her down!"

Luna thought, *Then I will live another thousand years!*

But Butterfly would need a LOT of support. Her friends were eager to help.

"Heave ho—up you go!"

They hoisted her food, water, a stove, fuel, and a tarp. She would need to tightly pack her waste in bags until her friends returned to haul it away.

That night, she slept under a tapestry of starlight.

The next morning, Butterfly
awoke to voices far below.

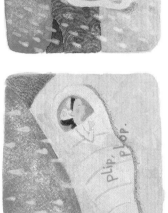

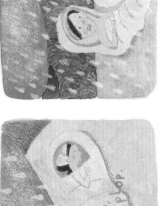

Up top, Butterfly held on tight to what SHE believed in—Luna.

But living 180 feet high in a tree wasn't easy. Her tree house was the size of a sandbox. She cooked all her food in one small pot.

And there wasn't a bathroom. She had to get creative. She collected rainwater to drink and bathe in. At first, raindrops popped like popcorn on her tarp roof, lulling her to sleep.

But soon, the refreshing rains grew into fierce storms.

Snap! CRACK! Flap. whoosh. creak. whirrrr. Rumble!

Butterfly could barely hold on. Lightning struck all around and thunder shook her courage. "I want to go home!" she yelled, but the howling wind swept her voice away.

Butterfly climbed inside her
cocoon and drifted to sleep.
In her dream, Luna spoke to her.

I'm frightened, Luna!

I will hold you
'til the sky is calm
and blue.

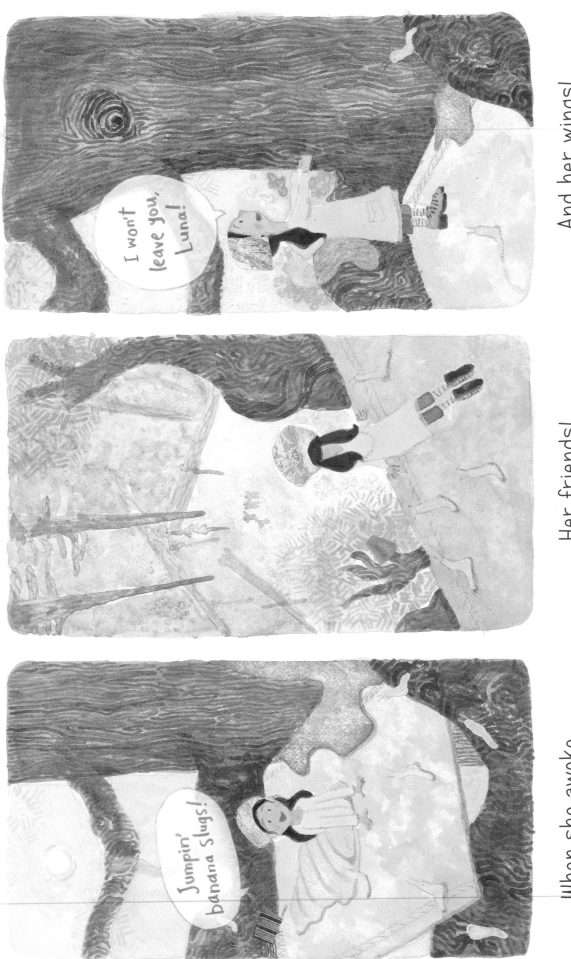

And her wings!

Her friends!

When she awoke,
she discovered the sun!

Butterfly kicked off her shoes and spent the day turning her tree house into a **home**.

To exercise, she climbed
barefoot to the very top
of Luna every morning.
With sticky, sappy feet,
she crawled like a spider
up and down Luna's trunk.

She explored
each branch and
met all her tree
mates.
And still, there
was more.

Deep within
Luna's split trunk,
Butterfly discovered
a magical cave.
It was alive!
   She found ferns,
huckleberry,
furry green moss,
tiny mushrooms,
bugs, chickadees,
hummingbirds,
chipmunks, and
even a fox!

"Luna!" Butterfly chirped.
"You are a forest within a forest!"
Luna beamed even brighter.
Butterfly knew what she had to do.

Her friends gathered supplies
she would need.
Solar-powered phone, check.
Hand-cranked solar radio, check.
Books about ancient forests, check.
Duct tape, check. Pens and paper
for writing letters, check.

Butterfly shared stories of Luna and the forest to anyone who would listen . . .

. . . and many people did. Busy days whirred and blurred into weeks and months and **a whole year.**

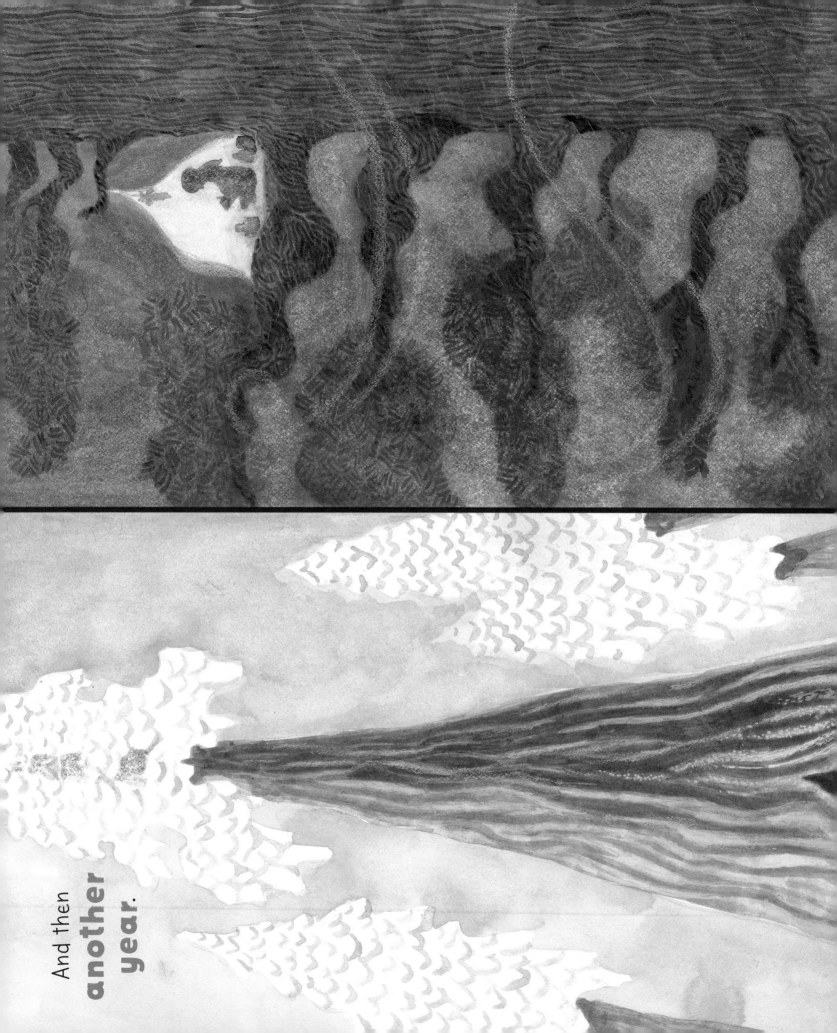

And then
**another
year.**

Butterfly worried,
"Will Luna ever be safe?"

But then, finally,
on the 738th day,
a message arrived!

Butterfly,
Luna is safe!

No one will cut
her down.
♡

Your friends

P.S. You can come
down now!

As her toes touched the soft earth,
Butterfly cried, "We did it, Luna!"
But she didn't want to leave her friend.
Butterfly hugged Luna good-bye and
heard Luna's voice in her heart:

As you grow strong
and tall toward the sun,
remember to bend with the wind.
And when you dream
and dance in the rain,

I'll be here
doing the same.

AUTHOR'S NOTE

Julia Butterfly Hill in Luna, 1998

IN 1996, WHEN JULIA BUTTERFLY HILL first stepped foot in the California redwood forest, she was overcome with awe by these ancient trees and the abundance of life within them. She soon learned that the majority of these 1,000- to 3,000-year-old trees had been logged for profit. Julia wanted to do something to help the trees left standing. She learned of tree-sitting, a peaceful act of civil disobedience in which a protester sits in a tree to protect it.

In October 1997, a forest activist from Earth First! free-climbed into an ancient redwood—Luna—to protect it from being cut down. Luna stands 200 feet tall near the top of a steep hillside. The tree's grove was marked for harvest by the Pacific Lumber Company. One year prior, the same logging company clear-cut a nearby hillside, which then crumbled in a mudslide, destroying many homes. Knowing the tree-sitter would not last long without a platform or supplies, a team of eleven fellow activists hiked up to Luna by the light of a full moon, climbed 180 feet into Luna's canopy, and secured a platform with ropes. It was on this night the group named the ancient redwood Luna and the famous tree-sit began.

During the first two months of the tree-sit, many people, including Julia Butterfly Hill, sat for a few days at a time in Luna's branches. Then, on December 10, 1997, Julia volunteered to sit in Luna for three to four weeks and, with the support of her ground team, ended up staying for two years. She was twenty-three years old.

Julia endured personal fears, intimidation from loggers, fierce storms, frostbite, and more. Despite these challenges, Julia remained in the tree, becoming a powerful voice for sustainable forestry and the integrity of the planet.

In December 1999, the Pacific Lumber Company and Julia Butterfly Hill signed an agreement to protect Luna and the surrounding grove. Sanctuary Forest, a nonprofit organization whose primary focus is land and water restoration and conservation, became entrusted with the responsibility of monitoring the Luna preserve in perpetuity. On December 18, 1999, after 738 days, Julia climbed down from Luna's arms. Since then, she has spent more than fifteen years as an inspirational speaker, teaching people about the environment and how to help preserve the earth for future generations.

Julia Butterfly Hill's peaceful activism and dedication to serving our earth inspires me deeply. After reading her memoir, *The Legacy of Luna: The Story of a Tree, a Woman, and the Struggle to Save the Redwoods*, I knew I wanted to make a picture book that would bring her courageous story to children. Her message is simple: each and every one of us can make a difference. I chose to tell of Julia's time in Luna in my own way—simplifying a very complex, intense, and political journey and depicting her as a girl. The essence of Julia's story remains; it is a story of strength, endurance, teamwork, commitment, and love. Luna still stands

to this day as a beacon of hope for the ancient forests, and Julia made that possible.

While working on the book, I had the opportunity to spend an enchanting day at the base of Luna, listening to many stories from Luna's caretaker, Stuart Moskowitz. My family and I camped in the redwoods—breathing deeply, lying on the forest floor, painting, and playing with banana slugs. Luna and the Redwood Forest fueled my illustrations with detail and magic.

For more information, or to donate to Sanctuary Forest, visit sanctuaryforest.org.

For the trees

A GIANT tree-hug to Patrick & Tulsi; Jo-Lynne Worley & Joanie Shoemaker; Connie Long; Stuart Moskowitz; my designer, April Ward; and my magical editor, Christy Ottaviano, for your cheerleading, creativity, and support in bringing this book to life!

This book was printed on paper from responsible, FSC®-certified sources.

Henry Holt and Company, LLC, *Publishers since 1866*
120 Broadway, New York, NY 10271 • mackids.com

Henry Holt® is a registered trademark of Henry Holt and Company, LLC.
Copyright © 2015 by Jenny Sue Kostecki-Shaw
"Redwood" song lyrics © Jenny Bird

Library of Congress Cataloging-in-Publication Data
Kostecki-Shaw, Jenny Sue, author, illustrator.
Luna and me : the true story of a girl who lived in a tree to save a forest / Jenny Sue Kostecki-Shaw. — First edition.
     pages   cm
Summary: "Social activism combines with environmentalism in this picture book bio of Julia Butterfly Hill and Luna, the thousand-year-old redwood tree whose life she saved" —Provided by publisher.
ISBN 978-0-8050-9976-8 (hardback)
1. Hill, Julia Butterfly—Juvenile literature. 2. Women conservationists—California—Humboldt County—Biography—Juvenile literature. 3. Luna (Calif. : Tree)—Juvenile literature. 4. Old growth forest conservation—California—Humboldt County—Juvenile literature. 5. Logging—California—Humboldt County—Juvenile literature. 6. Pacific Lumber Company—Juvenile literature. I. Title.
SD129.H53K67 2015   333.75097941'12—dc23   2014041427

Henry Holt books may be purchased for business or promotional use. For information on bulk purchases, please contact
the Macmillan Corporate and Premium Sales Department at (800) 221-7945 x5442 or by e-mail at specialmarkets@macmillan.com.

First Edition—2015 / Designed by April Ward

Acrylics, watercolors, salt, pencil, and collage on Strathmore illustration board were used to create the illustrations for this book.
Printed in China by RR Donnelley Asia Printing Solutions Ltd., Dongguan City, Guangdong Province

10